MW01229481

The Q

The Craziness

ur Memories

By Greg Muñoz

Cover Art by Niya Morton

This Journal Was Completed By:

_____

_____

_____

_____

This journal is dedicated to all those who were affected by the Pandemic of 2020.

We will never forget the bad,
but we will *always* remember the good.

Table of Contents

Introduction

What do you think of and feel when you hear words like "quarantine," "non-essential," and virtual classroom? Do you remember when you first heard about the pandemic? Did your place of work close? Were your children sent home from school? For most people in the world, the pandemic changed how life would be lived in the year 2020. For many, what began as a crisis became an opportunity for creativity and connection.

This journal was written so that you can capture the event and how it affected your life. There are prompts on the pages for you to journal your thoughts, and scattered blank pages for you to draw, scrapbook or write about things that are unique to your family. You will also find some fun family questions to stimulate conversations, as well as a place for your personal emergency pandemic plan.

It is my hope that this journal will give you a record of what life was like for you and the people you love, during this challenging period, and by reflecting, you will discover what was added to your life in a time when so much was taken away.

What words or phrases come to mind when you think of the pandemic of 2020?

You Record the Facts

Where did the pandemic start?

Where was the first outbreak?

Where did the first deaths occur?

Which was the first state in the USA to report a death from the virus?

What was the last state in the USA to report its first case of the virus?

What country reported the most deaths?

What was the total number of deaths in your city?

BREAKING NEWS

Write, draw, or paste news headlines here

What were your initial reactions when you heard about the pandemic?

What was your initial reaction to the shelter-in place rule?

When you realized the virus was serious and spreading, what was your reaction?

What were your biggest concerns/fears?

Personal Notes, Thoughts, Pictures or Drawings

What Do You Mean It's Not Essential?

Describe the effect the pandemic had on your job/business.

How did you cope with the changes?

Did you have to change how you earned an income? If so, describe that experience:

Were you told that your job/business was not essential? If so, describe your feelings/reaction:

Describe what lifestyle changes (if any) you had to make to accommodate changes in your income:

What were some of your favorite places and businesses that closed?

Personal Notes, Thoughts, Pictures or Drawings

Limit One Per Household!

Businesses in your area that were considered essential and allowed to stay open:

Businesses you <u>wished</u> were considered essential:

Items that were difficult to find in stores:

The silliest items you stocked:

What were the most essential items that you stocked?

Interesting or Funny
Photos or Images
Depicting this time period

Keep Your Distance Buddy!

What did your city do to enforce social distancing and what safety regulations did they implement?

How did you deal with social distancing & safety rules?

How did you acquire a facemask and how did you feel about wearing it?

How did you replace hugging or shaking hands with people?

What major events & special occasions were you unable to attend or host?

How did you celebrate major events & special occasions during social distancing?

How did you maintain your hair since all the salons were closed?

Who were the people you stayed connected with the most and why?

How did you stay connected?

Stay Home!
Save Lives!

What was the most difficult thing for your family during the crisis?

Being sheltered in place challenged (or forced) you to:

Things you really longed for:

How did you uplift and support one another while sheltered in place?

Upon reflection, what could you have handled better?

Did you lose anyone during the pandemic? If so, describe the experience and how you got through it:

Draw or write about your average day/routine:

Things you did as a family that you have never done before:

Rules/boundaries your family had to establish for peace and sanity:

How you kept yourselves entertained:

Hobbies/interests that you took up:

Things you did that weren't part of your normal routine:

Things you did to stay active:

Creative location(s)/activities that replaced the gym, sports practice, or work out classes:

New recipes you tried and fun meals you cooked:

How you stayed optimistic:

What you did (and didn't do) to stay positive and emotionally healthy:

What you learned to appreciate most while sheltered in place:

Things you and your family most looked
forward to doing when the
shelter-in-place was over:

What you did to help others:

Books you read:

Movies & shows that you watched:

Podcasts & music that you listened to:

Games & video games that you played:

Creative ideas, inventions, books, music etc. that you came up with:

Arts & crafts that you did:

New habits you developed:

What you learned about yourself:

How much weight you gained or lost:

What do you hope continues even when things go back to "normal"?

Personal Notes, Thoughts, Pictures or Drawings

Family Fun Activity

To get started, create a jar or basket full of numbers. To do this, write the numbers 1 through 56 on small pieces of paper. Put them in your container of choice. Each day take turns selecting a number. Have someone read the question that corresponds to the number drawn and everyone can take turns answering.

1. If I could be perfect at one thing, it would it be _____. Why?

2. If I could live anywhere, I would live _____. Why?

3. What is something that you're really afraid of?

4. What really makes/made you angry about the pandemic?

5. If you had all the time and money, where & how would you live?

6. What is your proudest accomplishment?

7. What is the best book you ever read and why?

8. What do you appreciate most about your family/spouse?

9. What movie made you cry and why?

10. When you were little, what did you want to be?

11. If you could be the best athlete, what would your sport be?

12. If you could drive any car for one day, what car would it be?

13. For $100, what would you choose to sing at Karaoke night?

14. Would you rather eat: a snail, half of a live lizard, a piece of a rattlesnake or a potato bug?

15. If you could hire someone to do one thing for you, what would it be?

16. If you could only eat one thing for the rest of your life, what would it be?

17. Where would you vacation for one month and why?

18   If money was no object, what would you do all day and with whom?

19.   If you could go back in time, where would you travel to and why?

20.   If you could play one instrument, what would it be and why?

21.   What is the best gift you have ever been given?

22.   What is the worst gift you have ever received?

23.   What is one thing that people do that irritates you the most?

24.   If you had a super-power what would it be and why?

25.   What three things would you do if you won the lottery?

26.   If you could hunt any animal, which would you choose?

27.   If you could change one event in history, what would it be?

28.   What's the worst movie you've ever watched?

29.   Would you rather be the most attractive or the smartest person on earth and why? (No, you can't have both)

30.   Have you ever secretly admired someone? Who was it?

31.   What's your favorite day of the year and why?

32.   What's the bravest thing you've ever done or seen done?

33.   What was the best book you read and why?

34.   What's your favorite dessert?

35.   If you could successfully teach people one thing, what would it be?

36.   Whose part would you want to play in the Wizard of Oz and why?

37.   What's your favorite fast food?

38.   If you had one last meal, what would you eat?

39.   What game would you take on a deserted island?

40. If you had one wish to be able to do any one thing for a day, what would it be?

41. How many Wonders of the World can you name?

42. What was/is a favorite childhood toy or game?

43. Where were you when you had your first kiss? How old were you? Who was it?

44. What's the worst thing you've ever eaten?

45. What would you say you're really good at?

46. What would you say you're not good at?

47. What would you like to be really good at?

48. Which famous person in the present or past would you like to meet and why?

49. What's the best joke you ever heard?

49. What one word would you use to describe your family?

50. Who was your favorite teacher in school and why?

51. If you could go back in time and change one thing you did, what would it be and why?

52. Who was your first crush on TV?

53. What was your first job?

54. If you could be the lead singer of any music group, which would it be?

55. What is your favorite family holiday tradition and why?

56. What family tradition do you wish you had?

Family
Pandemic Plan

List the people who have agreed to be responsible for the care of your children, pets, home, yourself, etc. in case you contract the virus:

1.   Name: _____

      Phone: _____

2.   Name: _____

      Phone: _____

3.   Name: _____

      Phone: _____

Have letters of authorization allowing caregivers to seek medical treatment for your children, yourself, and your pets. Have copies of insurance cards ready and other important medical documents the caregiver may need.

Use this page to provide allergy and medication information, dietary restrictions, physical restrictions or limitations, daily routine, and any other information that may help in providing care.

In case of relocation, pack a bag with overnight essentials and a copy of the special instructions from the previous page. Include favorites like a book, a toy, a photo, or anything else you think would bring comfort.

Final reflections on the pandemic and its impact on my family

Final reflections on the pandemic and its impact on my family

Made in the USA
Columbia, SC
27 June 2020

11281236R00035